110

Progressive Etudes

for

SNARE DRUM

BOOK ONE

No. 1 to 57

by

ROBERT W. BUGGERT

Contents

Whole Note Etude

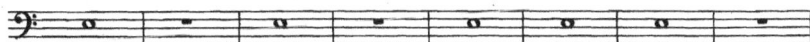

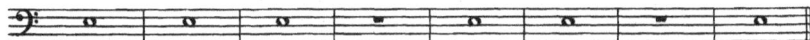

Whole Rest Etude

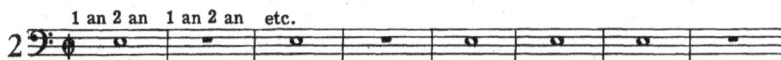

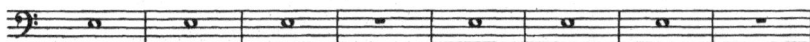

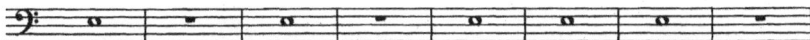

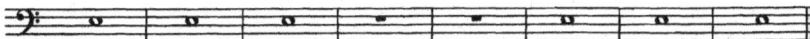

EL 333

Whole Note Whole Rest cont.

Whole Notes-Half Notes-Whole Rests

1 an 2 an etc.

5

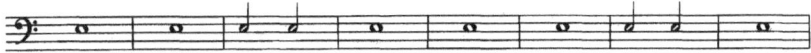

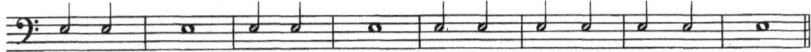

6

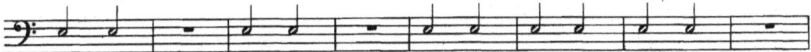

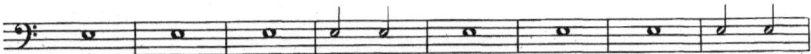

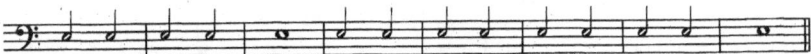

EL 333

6

7

8

EL 333

Whole Notes Half Notes
Whole Rests · Half Rests

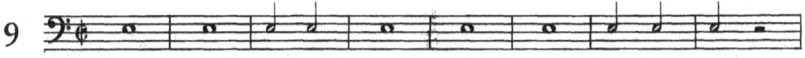

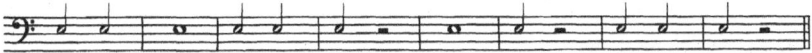

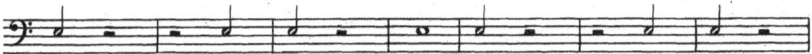

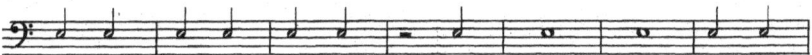

8

0

Etude for Whole Notes & Half Notes

EL 333

First Eight Measure Street Beats

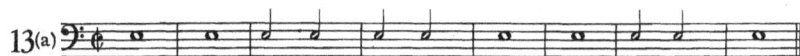

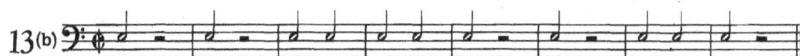

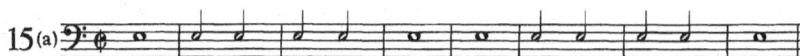

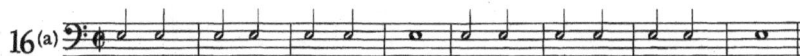

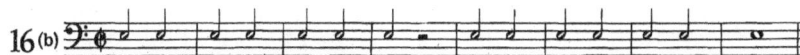

Introduction to Quarter Notes

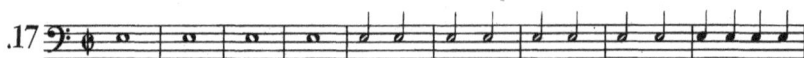

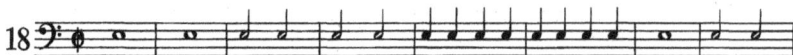

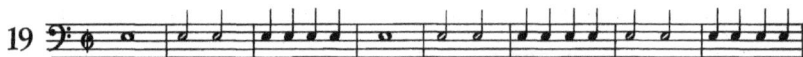

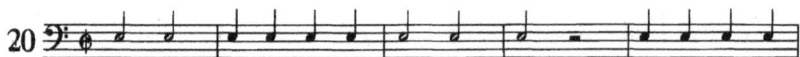

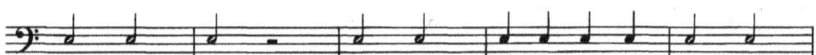

21

22

23

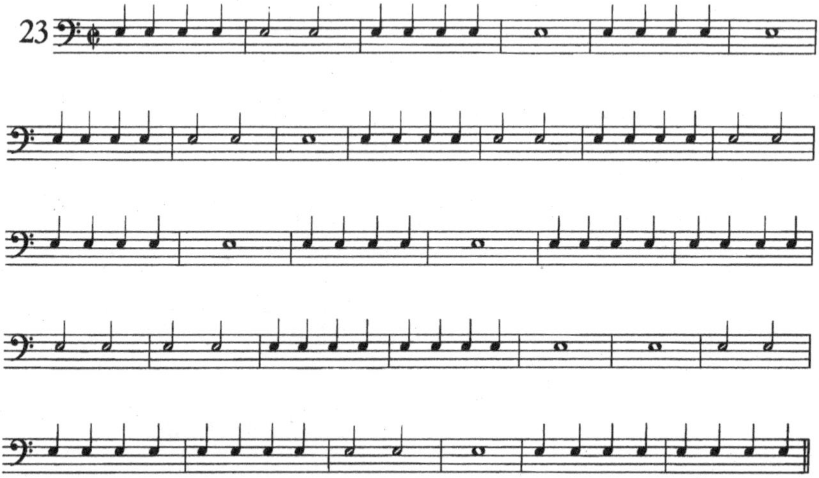

24

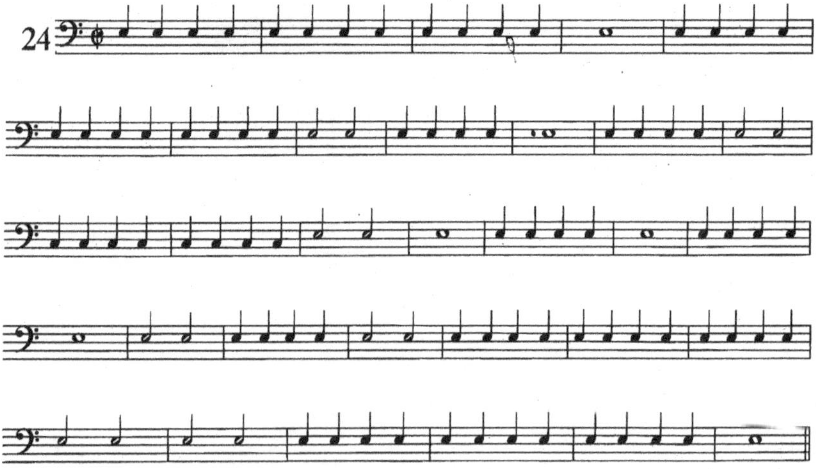

EL 333

27

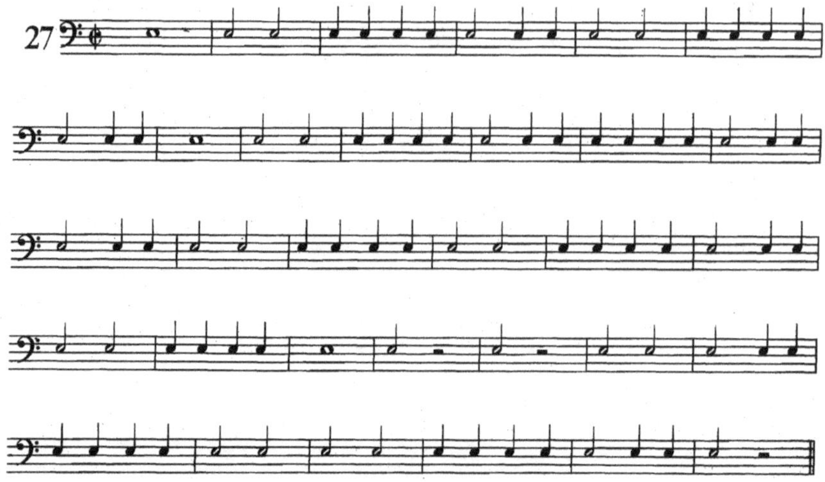

28

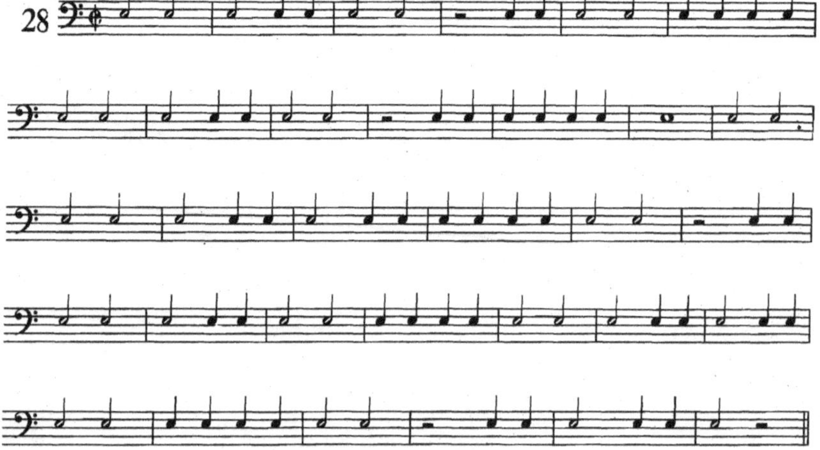

29

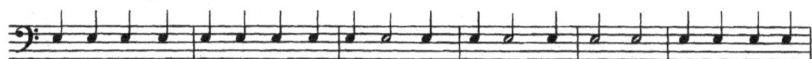

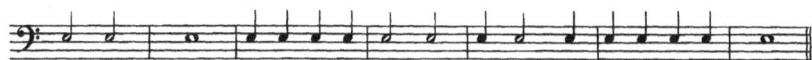

30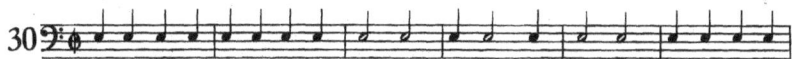

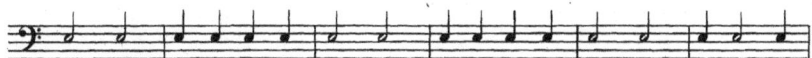

EL 333

31

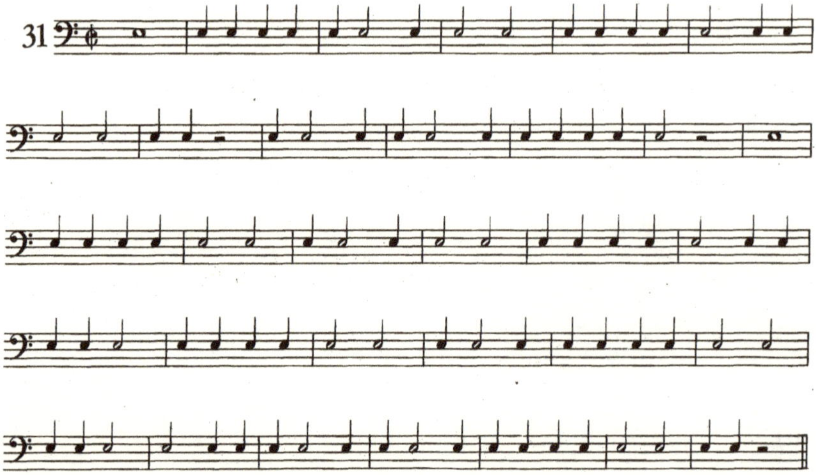

32

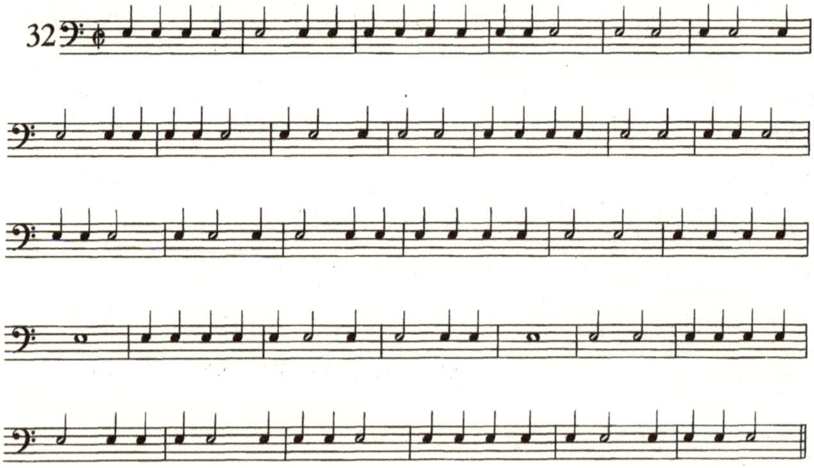

Review - All previously learned patterns combined.

Trio

Ten Street Beats

First Drum Solo

Quarter Notes & Quarter Rests

Study patterns

40

41

42

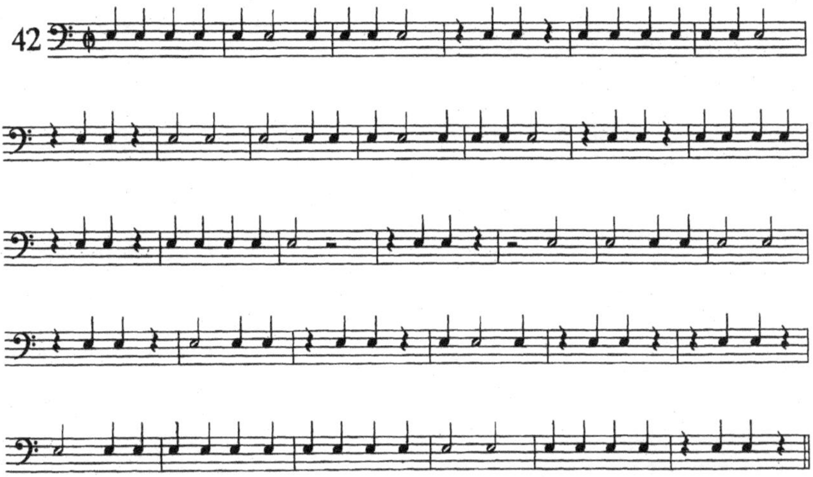

43

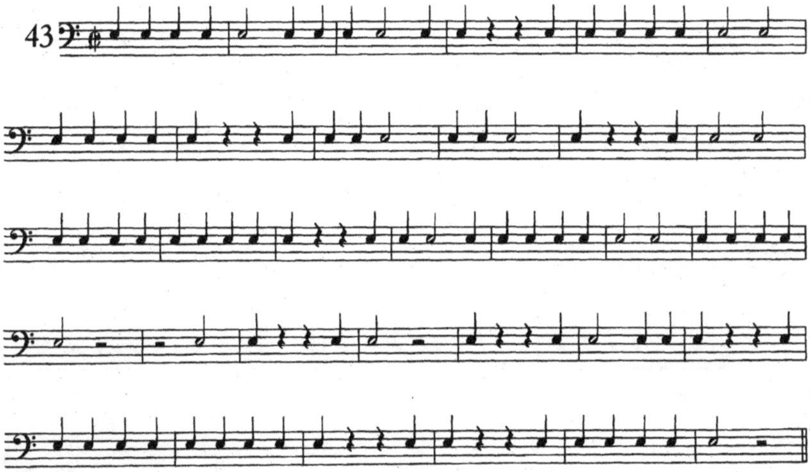

24

EL 333

Second Drum Solo

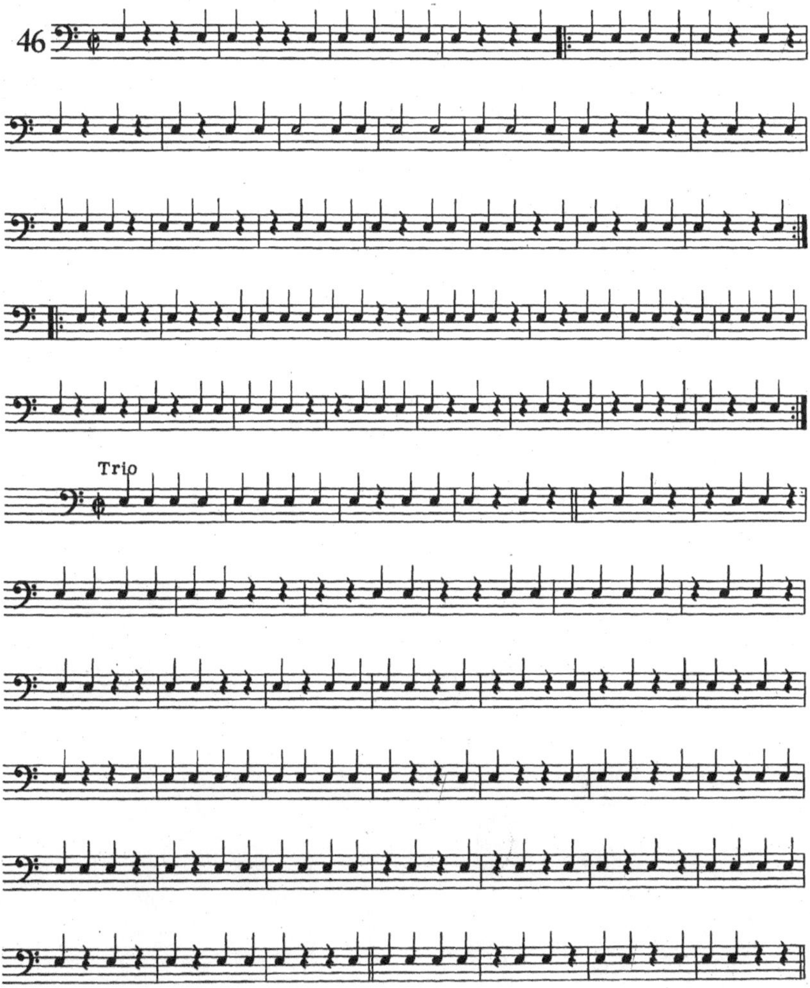

Street Beats

Eight Notes

28

EL 333

Syncopation

Eight Rests

Street Beats

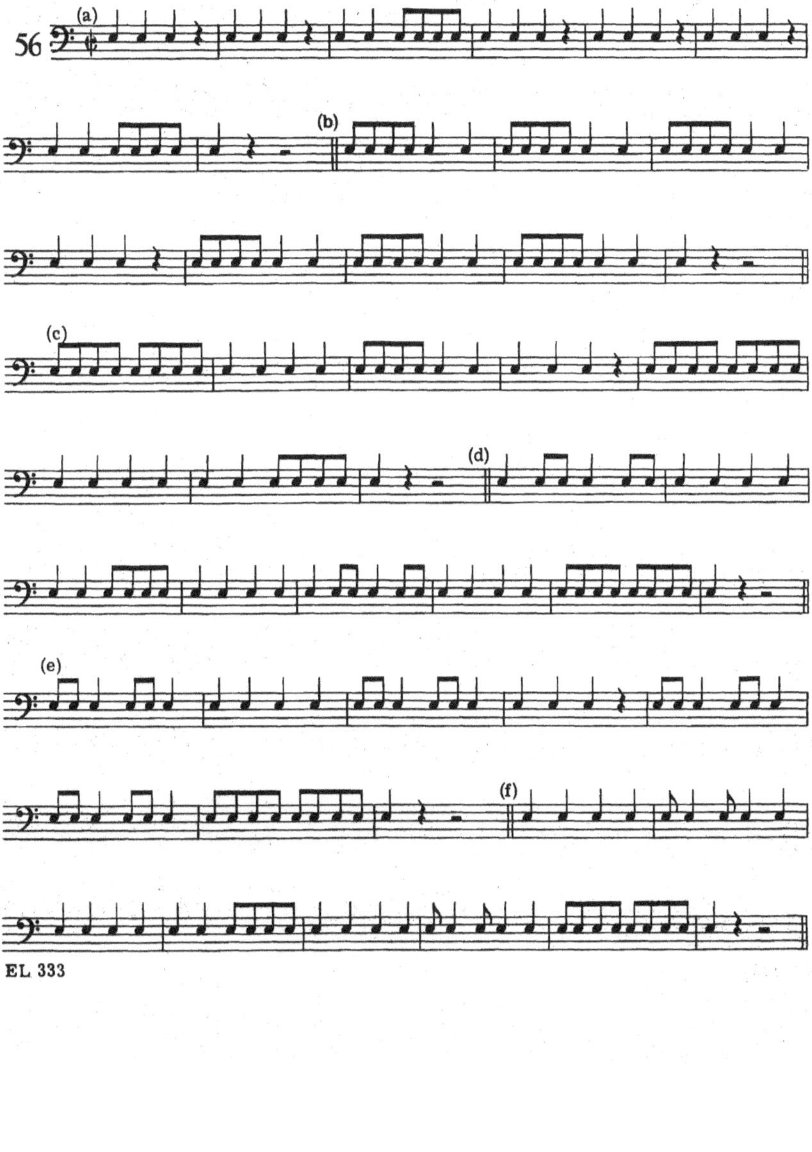

www.ingramcontent.com/pod-product-compliance
Lightning Source LLC
Chambersburg PA
CBHW031009090426
42737CB00008B/748